WALTER
WHITE

and the Power of Organized Protest

Robert E. Jakoubek

GATEWAY CIVIL RIGHTS
THE MILLBROOK PRESS
BROOKFIELD, CONNECTICUT

Library of Congress Cataloging-in-Publication Data
Jakoubek, Robert E.
Walter White and the power of organized protest / by
Robert E. Jakoubek.
p.   cm. — (Gateway civil rights)
Includes bibliographical references and index.
Summary: Relates the details of the life and career of the
black reporter and civil rights activist who became secretary of the NAACP.
ISBN 1-56294-378-2 (Lib. bdg.) ISBN 1-56294-697-8 (pbk.)
1. White, Walter Francis, 1893–1955—Juvenile literature.   2. Afro-Americans—Biography—Juvenile literature.   3. Civil rights workers—United States—Biography—Juvenile literature.   4. National Association for the
Advancement of Colored People—Biography—Juvenile
literature.   5. Afro-Americans—Civil rights—Juvenile
literature.   6. Civil rights movements—United States—
History—20th century—Juvenile literature.   [1. White,
Walter Francis, 1893–1955.   2. Civil rights workers.
3. Afro-Americans—Biography.   4. National Association for the Advancement of Colored People.   5. Afro-
Americans—Civil rights.   6. Civil rights movements—
History.]   I. Title.   II. Series.
E185.97.W6J34   1994
323′.092—dc20   [B]   93-8715   CIP   AC

Photographs courtesy of Bettmann: cover, pp. 26, 27;
Wide World Photos: cover inset, pp. 2–3, 16, 23, 29, 30;
Library of Congress: pp. 1, 4, 13, 25; *Atlanta Journal-
Constitution:* p. 7; Brown Brothers: pp. 9, 14; Amistad
Research Center: p. 11; Gumby Collection, Columbia
University: p. 15; The Schomburg Center for Research
in Black Culture: p. 21.

Published by The Millbrook Press
2 Old New Milford Road, Brookfield, Connecticut 06804

Protesters march in Washington, D.C., in 1946,
outraged by the lynchings of blacks in Georgia.

Young *Walter White* enjoyed few things more than riding with his father through the streets of his hometown, Atlanta, Georgia. George White was a mailman who traveled along a set route every afternoon. Walter was nearly always at his father's side. As their little horse-drawn cart, piled high with the day's mail, bounced and swayed along, father and son sat close together on the buggy's narrow front seat discussing everything under the sun.

One sultry September afternoon in 1906, when Walter was thirteen, he and his father set out on their usual route. George White was worried. The threat of mob violence hung in the air.

All through that steaming hot summer, trouble between blacks and whites in Atlanta had been in the making. The bitter campaign for governor of Georgia had whipped up a frenzy among whites. Each of the candidates in the race promised to limit the rights of black Georgians. They pledged to stop blacks from voting. They called for new and stronger laws of segregation, or the separation of the races. Blacks and whites, they boomed, must be kept apart in public places.

At nearly every street corner, Walter and his father saw sour-looking white men clustering together. As they made their way to a mailbox on the corner of Peachtree and Houston, there suddenly came a roar louder than any Walter had ever heard.

A mob was on the march. For the next four days Atlanta would be in the grip of a race riot. As many as fifty blacks would die in the violence.

In the downtown section, throngs of whites cursed, threatened, and chased any African American who happened to be on the streets. On Peachtree Street, Walter and his father heard a terrifying cry. Then they saw hobbling toward them a lame black man who shined shoes at a nearby barber shop. Dozens of whites surrounded the crippled man, clubbed him to the ground, and kicked him to death.

Around the corner, whites were chasing an elderly black woman whom Walter and George recognized as the cook at a local hotel. She ran to their cart, pleading for help. "Father handed the reins to me," Walter remembered years later, "and though he was of slight stature, reached down and lifted the woman into the cart." Walter lashed the horse, and the cart with its three passengers sped off to safety.

During the first day of the frightful riot, the mobs left the Whites alone. They were, like millions of American families, of mixed racial heritage. Both of Walter's parents were partly African American. Yet they were light skinned. From his mother, Walter inherited blue eyes and blond hair. Some fair-skinned African Americans tried to "pass" for white to avoid the hardships suffered by black people. The Whites never considered

Headlines such as these, appearing in The Atlanta Constitution *the morning after the 1906 Atlanta race riot began, did nothing to calm either blacks or whites. In fact, the riot continued for three more days.*

doing this. They were proud to be African Americans, and they lived in the black section of Atlanta.

On the second night of rioting the mob began marching through Atlanta's black neighborhoods, heading right toward the Whites' house on Houston Street. George White ordered his wife and daughters to the rear of the house. He and Walter, armed with pistols they had borrowed from friends, crouched down in the darkened windows facing the street.

Around midnight the torchlight-carrying mob moved in. "That's where that nigger mail carrier lives!" screamed a voice from the street. "Let's burn it down!"

George turned to Walter: "Son, don't shoot until the first man puts his foot on the lawn and then—don't you miss!"

As Walter watched the mob closing in, any doubts about his identity vanished—and vanished for good. "I knew then who I was," he would write later; "I was a Negro, a human being with an invisible pigmentation which marked me a person to be hunted, hanged, abused, discriminated against, kept in poverty and ignorance."

As Walter and his father aimed their pistols, shots rang out from down the street. The mob stopped in its tracks. Some turned and fled. Others headed toward the sound of the gunfire. But no one stepped onto the Whites' front lawn.

Their lives and home had been saved. Walter had learned the lesson of his life. He had learned what it meant to be hated. He would spend his life trying to help those whose experience mirrored his own.

The presence of armed soldiers on the streets of Atlanta eventually brought the rioting mobs under control.

"Using Your Heart and Brains"

Walter White was born on July 1, 1893. All his life he had tremendous energy. Once, in his early thirties, he wrote a novel of over 60,000 words in less than two weeks. As a boy growing up in his hometown, Atlanta, Georgia, he was forever on the go.

At ten he got his first job, working in a tailor's shop. Two years later he went on to become a bellboy at the Piedmont Hotel downtown. Walter also attended school longer than most boys in his neighborhood. The state of Georgia did not provide public high schools for black children. Most of them went to separate black schools that ended with the eighth grade. But Walter's parents insisted he continue. They scrimped and saved so that he could attend the private high school for blacks run by Atlanta University, a mostly black college.

In 1912 he started college at Atlanta University. Once more, he was a man in motion. "In addition to playing not too good football," he recalled, "serving as president of my class, being a member of the debating team, and a few other extracurricular activities, I worked throughout the school year." Upon graduating in 1916 Walter White, at age twenty-three, went to work as a clerk for the Standard Life Insurance Company.

An 1899 sketch of Atlanta University, where Walter White received his college degree.

White impressed his bosses and was quickly promoted to the better-paying post of cashier. He might have had a long, steady career in insurance. As it turned out, though, his stay in the world of claims and policies was brief.

The whites in Atlanta were set on making it tough for blacks to have an education. In 1914 the city's board of education dropped the eighth grade from the black public schools. Two years later they announced plans to drop the seventh grade. With the money saved on the black schools, the board announced, they would build a new all-white high school.

The African Americans of Atlanta were outraged, none more than Walter White. A group of young blacks decided to fight back. White wrote a letter to the national headquarters of the National Association for the Advancement of Colored People (NAACP). Founded in 1909 by both blacks and whites, the organization was leading the fight for the rights of black Americans. Both its national headquarters in New York City and its local chapters throughout the country tried to aid African Americans who had been unfairly treated.

With the encouragement of the NAACP, White and some others presented their case to the school board. It was one of the first times Atlanta's blacks had stood up to the powerful white establishment. To their astonishment and delight, the protest succeeded. Several members of the board changed their minds, and the seventh grade was restored to the black schools.

Seeing what could be done by organizing, White helped establish an Atlanta chapter of the NAACP. In December 1916 he was elected its secretary. His good work did not escape the notice of the NAACP's national office. James Weldon Johnson, the organization's field secretary, was particularly impressed. In early 1918 he asked White if he would like the job of assistant secretary in the New York headquarters.

Johnson's offer came as a bolt out of the blue. The NAACP position meant less money, moving to New York, and an un-

Secretary Walter White (seated at far right) and his fellow officers of the Atlanta chapter of the NAACP in 1917.

certain future. Undecided, White talked it over with his father. As they had done so many times before, they hitched up the horse and went for a long ride. George White quietly told his son what he should do: "Your mother and I have given you the best education we could afford, and a good Christian home training. Fortunately, it is better than most colored children have

James Weldon Johnson, of the NAACP's national office, was so impressed with White that he offered him a job in the NAACP's New York office. The move was an important step in White's career.

had. Now it is your duty to pass on what you have been given by helping others less fortunate to get a chance in life. I don't want to see you go away. I'll miss you. But remember always, God will be using your heart and brains to do His will.''

Into the Fire

A few months before his twenty-fifth birthday, Walter White, the NAACP's new assistant secretary, moved into a furnished room in a boarding house in Harlem, New York's main black section. He discovered his landlady knew the recipes for ninety-two soups. In the years he lived there, he never grew tired of her cooking nor decided which of the ninety-two was most delicious. It was good he liked soup; his starting salary with the NAACP was only $1,200 a year.

Low pay was the least of his concerns. His job at the NAACP was very dangerous. For ten years, from 1918 through

1928, White led forty-one inquiries into the lynchings, or mob killings, of African Americans. Most took place in the Deep South, and sometimes he came face-to-face with death.

In 1917, the year before White moved to New York, more than fifty African Americans were lynched. Most often these lynchings took place in the rural South, at night, and attracted little notice. The NAACP wanted to bring lynching into the light of day, to shock the nation with the truth.

The NAACP decided White was the perfect man for the job. He was smart, energetic, reliable, and brave. And he looked white. With his blond hair, blue eyes, and convincing Georgia drawl, he could move freely among southern whites. To him a white person would open up, perhaps telling the truth about a lynch mob.

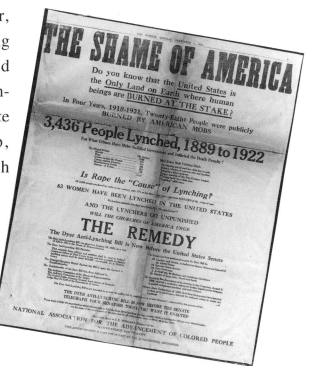

In an attempt to educate the public, White directed the NAACP's antilynching campaign to pay for newspaper ads like this one.

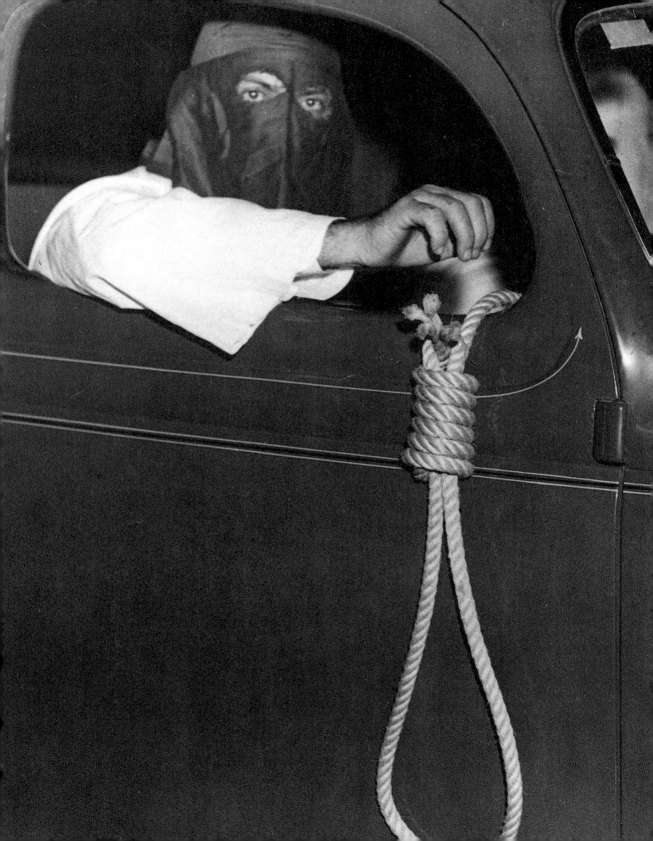

LYNCHING

The number of lynchings reported between 1882 and 1962 is shocking. Of the nearly 5,000 people who were killed in all, about 3,500 of these were black. In 1892 alone there were 230 victims, 161 of whom were black.

Principles of law and order were swept aside. A mob would track down, capture, and kill a person who may have been accused of a crime but had not yet been arrested. The victim had no chance to defend himself.

Sometimes the victim was dragged out of a jail cell, where he awaited trial. Often he was innocent of the crime. Assuming his guilt, the mob would put him to death, usually by hanging.

Nearly all lynch mobs went scot-free. Local sheriffs and police, nearly always white, had little interest in catching the murderers of blacks. In 1938, *Time* magazine reported that "after 99.4 percent of U.S. lynchings, sheriffs had reported . . . no arrests, no indictments, no convictions."

Gradually, the number of lynchings declined. In 1947, for instance, there was only one documented lynching. In 1962, there were none.

In the late summer of 1919, the NAACP sent him on a mission to Phillips County, Arkansas, where seventy-nine blacks had been sentenced to either death or long terms in prison. Newspapers carried wild stories about ''black riots'' in which white men had been killed. White's job was to find out the truth.

Along the way he stopped in Little Rock, the capital of Arkansas, and arranged for a meeting with the governor. Posing as a white reporter for the *Chicago Daily News,* he quickly won the governor's confidence. In his big, high ceilinged office, the governor leaned back and casually put down the NAACP and defended the ''good white people of Arkansas.'' As they parted, he handed White a letter of introduction to be used in case White ran into trouble in Phillips County.

The governor's letter magically opened doors. White saw and talked with all sorts of people in Phillips County. Gradually, he pieced together the story of what had really happened:

A group of black sharecroppers—poor tenant farmers who worked land owned by whites—had tried to form an organization to help each other. Just when they began their meeting in a small country church, a white mob armed with guns attacked. Bullets flew into the church and killed several blacks. A few sharecroppers fired back, and one of the white gunmen fell dead.

The shooting of the white man triggered an antiblack bloodbath. Gangs of whites swept across the county, lynching any African American they could catch. White sadly discovered that more than two hundred blacks had died in the massacre. Hundreds more fled the county. Others were rounded up and forced to work the farmland of whites for no money.

Seventy-nine black men refused to flee or to work for whites without pay. They were placed on trial for "murder and insurrection." Declared guilty, sixty-seven were sentenced to prison and twelve to death by hanging.

Having learned the gruesome truth, White nearly became a victim himself. Evidently, he had asked a few too many questions. His real identity had been discovered. A local black man took him aside and alerted him to the danger. "I don't know what you are down here for," he whispered, "but I just heard them talking about you—I mean the white folks—and they say they are going to get you."

White hurried to the railroad station. He made it just in time. A train was pulling in, and he leaped aboard. As he was buying a ticket to Memphis, the conductor suggested he should stay in town. The "fun" was about to begin. "There's a yellow nigger down here passing for white and the boys are going to get him," the conductor said.

"What'll they do with him?" White asked, trying to appear as innocent as possible.

"When they get through with him he won't pass for white no more!" the conductor replied.

White made it home safely and wrote for the *Chicago Daily News* the whole shocking story of the Phillips County massacre. The response was immediate; the NAACP received donations and pledges of support from all over the country. Taking up the cause of the seventy-nine convicted blacks, the organization appealed their case all the way to the Supreme Court of the United States. On February 19, 1923, the Court reversed the convictions of all seventy-nine men. "Against unbelievable odds," White wrote later, "we had won!"

White continued to investigate and expose the crime of lynching. In speeches and newspaper and magazine articles he told the nation about the terrible, violent attacks on innocent African Americans. His 1924 novel, *The Fire in the Flint,* was a moving account of a young black doctor who was lynched after being falsely accused of a crime. In 1929 he published *Rope and Faggot: A Biography of Judge Lynch.* The book quickly won respect as a thorough, thoughtful study of lynching. "This book should be read by every citizen of the United States," the lawyer Clarence Darrow said. "It might possibly do them some good."

White's crusade against lynching advanced him to the very front ranks of the NAACP. In 1930, a year after James Weldon Johnson stepped down from his post, White became acting secretary. The following year, he was promoted to secretary, the organization's leading position.

The Most
Potent Leader

By the late 1930s Walter White had become one of America's most famous people. He was awarded the Spingarn Medal in 1937 for his tireless efforts to help black Americans. In 1938 his picture appeared on the cover of *Time* magazine. Inside, *Time* proclaimed that his crusade against lynching had made "spunky, dapper forty-four-year-old Negro White the most potent leader of his race in the U.S."

Within the boundaries of a racist, segregated society, White had done well for himself. He and his first wife, Leah Gladys, and their two children lived in a spacious five-room apartment in the best building on the best street in the best black neighborhood in New York City.

As secretary of the NAACP, White missed no chance to champion the cause of African Americans. "The Negro would never be even where he is today," said a black leader in the late 1940s, "if Walter hadn't always been in there fighting, and what's more, always waging the frontal attack."

The "frontal attack" of White's NAACP took place mainly in the nation's courtrooms. White was convinced that the legal system offered African Americans their best hope of overturning racism. At his direction, the NAACP expanded its legal staff and its challenges to segregation. From the mid-1930s

Throughout the 1930s and 1940s, Walter White spoke frequently and eloquently to further the cause of African Americans.

through the 1950s, the NAACP's legal department scored many victories. It successfully challenged restrictions on the right of blacks to vote in the South. It helped end segregation in transportation and housing. Its greatest triumphs were in the field of education. Over the years and through dozens of courts, the NAACP led the battle against separate, segregated schooling for blacks.

THURGOOD MARSHALL

In 1967, President Lyndon B. Johnson appointed Thurgood Marshall Associate Justice of the U.S. Supreme Court. Marshall became the first African American to join the high court. At the time of his appointment, a prominent journalist examined the career of the new justice. "In three decades," he wrote of Marshall, "he has probably done as much to transform the life of his people as any Negro alive today."

For twenty-five years, from 1936 until 1961, Marshall had been a lawyer for the NAACP. In 1938, he became head of its legal staff. With Walter White's support, Marshall and his NAACP lawyers used the legal process to fight the system of racial segregation.

He was remarkably successful. Twenty-nine times Marshall and the NAACP won victories when the Supreme Court decided in their favor. One by one these Supreme Court decisions struck down practices that discriminated against blacks in housing, education, voting practices, and transportation. Their greatest triumph came in 1954 in the famous case *Brown* v. *Board of Education of Topeka*. By a unanimous vote, the Supreme Court declared the practice of racial segregation in public education illegal. The *Brown* case changed things forever in the United States. The days of legal segregation were clearly coming to an end.

Marshall served on the Supreme Court from 1967 until his retirement at the age of eighty-three in 1991. He died in January 1993.

Thurgood Marshall (right) had White's complete support as he led the NAACP's legal battle against segregation.

During this period, White was a regular visitor at the White House. As the United States entered World War II, in 1941, he and the black union leader A. Philip Randolph pressured President Franklin D. Roosevelt to ban racial discrimination in the nation's defense industries. The president also established a Fair Employment Practices Commission, an agency that tried to curb discrimination in government jobs.

During the war, White traveled around the world looking into the treatment of black soldiers. They were in segregated troops, and he was not surprised that they were much worse off than other soldiers. White published his findings in a 1945 book, *A Rising Wind.* The book helped to move the president who followed Roosevelt, Harry S. Truman, to issue the 1948 order to desegregate the nation's armed forces.

In 1946, White had convinced Truman to appoint a special Committee on Civil Rights. Eventually, the committee issued a report entitled *To Secure the Rights,* which called for sweeping new civil rights laws.

Picketers protesting the "Jim Crow Army," which tolerated—and even encouraged— discrimination and segregation.

In 1946, Walter White (third from right) met with President Harry Truman (center) to discuss legislation against mob violence.

In the late 1940s, White began running into trouble at the NAACP. Since taking over he had run the organization in a firm, often willful, way. He had made enemies. In 1949 the association voted to limit his authority. He remained secretary, but he was no longer fully in charge.

Nor was he in the best of health. The endless activity—the years of travel, of speaking, and of writing—had worn him down. In 1947, when he was fifty-four, he had suffered a massive heart attack. He had recovered, but not to full strength. On March 21, 1955, he suffered a second heart attack. This time it was fatal.

More than three thousand people gathered for his funeral. His long struggle for justice would not be forgotten. "As long as history lasts," said Congressman Adam Clayton Powell, Jr., "and there is the cry for full human freedom, Walter White's name will be echoed down the corridors of time."

IMPORTANT DATES IN THE LIFE OF WALTER WHITE

1893   Walter White is born in Atlanta, Georgia, on July 1.

1906   A race riot breaks out in Atlanta on September 24.

1916   White graduates from Atlanta University.

1918   White moves to Harlem and becomes assistant secretary for the National Association for the Advancement of Colored People (NAACP), a position he will hold until 1928.

1924   White publishes a novel, *The Fire in the Flint.*

1929   White publishes a study of lynching, *Rope and Faggot: A Biography of Judge Lynch.*

1931   White becomes secretary of the NAACP.

1945   White publishes *A Rising Wind,* a book about discrimination against black soldiers in the U.S. Army.

1948   President Harry S. Truman desegregates the U.S. armed forces.

1955   Walter White dies from a heart attack on March 21.

FIND OUT MORE ABOUT WALTER WHITE AND HIS TIMES

The Civil Rights Movement in America from 1865 to the Present by Patricia and Fredrick McKissack (Chicago: Childrens Press, 1987).

Ida B. Wells-Barnett and the Antilynching Crusade by Suzanne Freedman (Brookfield, Conn.: The Millbrook Press, 1993).

Thurgood Marshall and Equal Rights by Seamus Cavan (Brookfield, Conn.: The Millbrook Press, 1993).

Walter White by Alison Fraser (New York: Chelsea House Publishers, 1991).

Walter White's antidiscrimination activities kept him in the public's eye right up to the end of his career. Here he pickets in front of a restaurant in 1951, four years before his death.

INDEX

Page numbers in *italics* refer to illustrations.